D1783847

POCKET IMAGES

Around Thatcham

POCKET IMAGES

Around Thatcham

Peter Allen

NONSUCH

First published 1992
This new pocket edition 2007

Nonsuch Publishing Limited
Cirencester Road, Chalford
Stroud, Gloucestershire, GL6 8PE
www.nonsuch-publishing.com

Nonsuch Publishing is an imprint of NPI Media Group

British Library Cataloguing in Publication Data.
A catalogue record for this book is available from the British Library.

ISBN 978-1-84588-464-2

Typesetting and origination by NPI Media Group
Printed in Great Britain

Contents

Harts Hill Road, 1904. A view of the one-time country lane leading from Thatcham to Bucklebury in the early years of the present century. On the left is the entrance to Harts Hill Farm.

Introduction

Thatcham, like Topsy, has just 'grow'd and grow'd'. In the summer of 1989 it was one of the places featured in a Sunday supplement article entitled 'Urban Overspill'. The distinction was a dubious one, for the article's subtitle was 'The Destruction of the British Countryside'. Thatcham has borne the brunt of the phenomenon, which began in the 1960s, whereby large numbers of people move from Britain's big cities to expanding settlements in 'urban villages'.

Yet it was not always so. For generations Thatcham was a sleepy rural community which the world passed by. True, settlers came here in the Middle Stone Age and in the Roman period but they left few traces of their presence. Similarly, little evidence remains of the former Saxon settlement, although these residents did leave one lasting memorial, the name of the place, 'Tace's-ham', the home of the Saxon chief Tace.

At the time of the Domesday Survey, when the population numbered perhaps 250, Thatcham was in the ascendant. There was a royal 'manor' (parish) of Thatcham, which lent its name to an extensive 'hundred' (administrative area). Thatcham hundred was only second (to Windsor) out of a total of thirty-two hundreds in Berkshire. Indeed, during the Middle Ages Thatcham went on to become one of only four 'boroughs' in the county.

Medieval Thatcham was a small market town with a population in the region of five hundred inhabitants. The market was certainly operating by the reign of King Henry I (maybe earlier). In 1222, during the reign of King Henry III, Thatcham was granted an annual two-day fair. Sadly, Thatcham's economic prosperity was eventually stifled by the emergence of its near-neighbour Newbury as the dominant market town in this part of Berkshire.

For the next five centuries Thatcham was merely an agricultural village—for most of this time the only industry in the place worthy of mention was wood-turning. When Queen Victoria came to the throne in 1837 the population had increased to about two-and-a-half thousand. Village life centred on the Broadway, with its green, and that part of the main London–Bath road (Chapel Street/High Street) at the top of it.

In the early twentieth century a flower show was held every August, the first parish hall was built in 1907, and a public fountain (with horse trough!) erected in 1911. Two world wars came and went without making any real impact on Thatcham, although a new military depot became G45, the US Army's largest G-depot in Britain between 1942 and 1946.

Thatcham began to expand during the inter-war years as ribbon development spread outwards from the old village centre along the main road, the A4. But it was in the post-war period that residential development escalated and housing estates mushroomed. Green fields gave way to red-brick development. As late as 1961 there were still only 2,300 households in Thatcham, but by 1981 the figure had passed the 5,000 mark. A mere six years later the number had rocketed to over 7,000 households.

When Queen Elizabeth II came to the throne in 1952, Thatcham was already one of the largest villages in the country. Its population boomed, from 4,788 in 1951 to 7,483 in 1961 and on to 10,592 in 1971. Under the terms of the Local Government Act of 1972 the parish council designated itself a town council from April 1974. Thatcham's population was 14,779 by 1981 and had reached 21,000 by the time of the 1991 census.

Today Thatcham claims to be 'the growth town of West Berkshire'. However, since the opening of the M4 motorway and the creation of a fast rail link with London, Thatcham has become something of a dormitory town. Many of the people who live here have little idea of the history of their adoptive home. Even the younger generations of long-standing Thatcham families have limited knowledge of the past character of their birthplace. The rate of change during the last thirty years can justly be described as 'dramatic'.

If there is a town in West Berkshire which needs its own photographic record, that town must surely be Thatcham. It is fortunate, therefore, that there are sources available to draw on. From private collections of both postcard views and family photographs it is possible to reconstruct images of Thatcham in days gone by. The views included in this book have been drawn together to portray the various aspects of village life as it used to be.

I am grateful to all those individuals (listed on the Acknowledgements page) who loaned me photographs for copying, and who supplied information about the people and places shown. I trust that they will find my selection and organization of the pictures acceptable. Above all, I hope that everyone who looks at the pictures will enjoy their glimpse of 'Thatcham in Old Photographs' as much as I enjoyed compiling it.

Peter Allen
Thatcham, 1992

One

Street Scenes

VIEW FROM CHURCH TOWER   Thatcham

View from the church tower (c. 1900) looking north-east across the nucleus of the old village of Thatcham. The houses are located on either side of the Broadway, or Broad Street as it used to be known. The large building in the centre of the picture is the Infants' School, used as such between 1828 and 1964.

Bath Road, the main road through Thatcham, looking east towards the village centre, *c.* 1915. Henwick Lanes leads off northwards.

Bath Road, c. 1915. Another view of the main road, near Bourne Arch, showing early twentieth-century ribbon development.

Bath Road, *c.* 1910. Among the houses on the north side of the A4 are six matching pairs of semis known as the 'twelve apostles'.

Newtown, Thatcham

Bath Road, c. 1910. 'Newtown' is a reminder that this part of Thatcham was once a satellite community to the village proper.

High Street, c. 1930. The building (centre) was the premises of Gush's Road Transport Service Ltd until demolition in 1934.

High Street, c. 1930. J. C. Norris, Fishmonger and Fruiterer kept a shop here but it was demolished in 1934 to permit road widening.

High Street with Church Lane leading off right and the original entrance to Park Lane leading off left, c. 1930.

HIGH ST THATCHAM

Another view along the High Street, then the main London–Bristol road, from outside The Cricketers' Arms, c. 1930.

Park Lane, looking north, c. 1913. The houses on the right are much the same today but the road now carries heavy traffic.

Park Lane, looking south towards the original junction with the High Street. The road is quiet in this bygone view.

High Street, looking east, c. 1915. The High Street becomes Chapel Street at the top of the Broadway (on the right).

High Street, looking west from the top of the Broadway, c. 1915. To the left is the White Hart Hotel.

Chapel Street, c. 1930, where the main road sweeps round the Broadway Corner, past Ashman's shop (now demolished).

Chapel Street, c. 1960. When the road was widened, the houses on the right lost their small front gardens.

Chapel Street with the old Wheatsheaf inn (demolished and rebuilt in 1927) visible on the right, c. 1910.

Chapel Street, looking westwards, c. 1930. On the right are the Thatched Cottages.

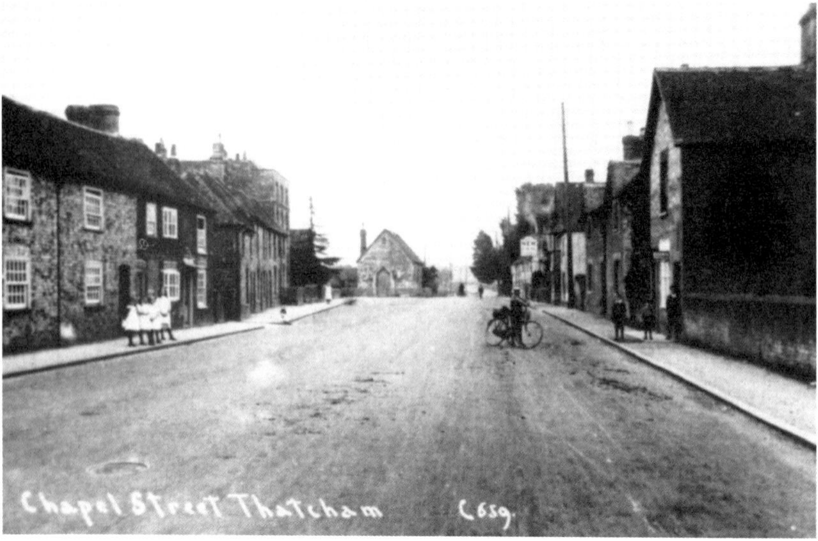
Chapel Street Thatcham
C659.

Chapel Street, looking east where it becomes London Road, c. 1915. The New Inn (right) is today the Prancing Horse.

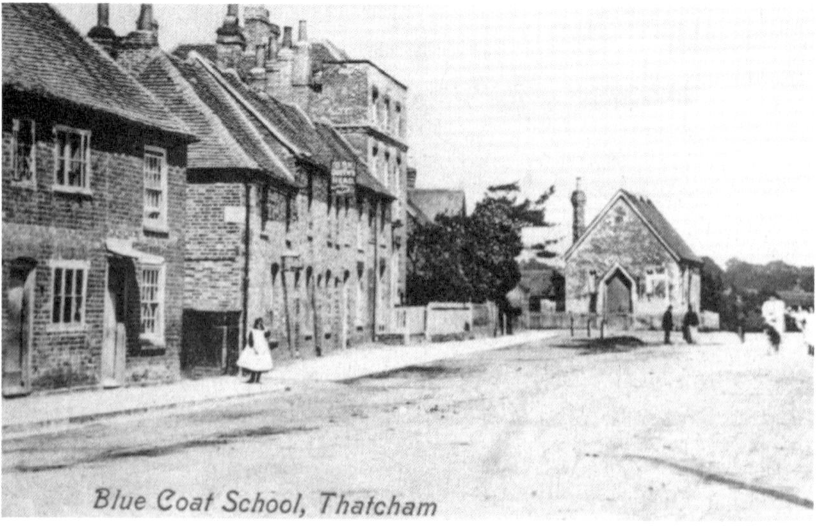
Blue Coat School, Thatcham

Chapel Street, featuring the long-gone Queen's Head inn in the row of buildings on the left, c. 1910.

London Road, leading towards Reading, c. 1940. It is bordered on the left by The Marsh (now known as Dunstan Green).

London Road, c. 1915. There was once a pond on The Marsh. In the background is the Plough inn, adjacent to Stoney Lane.

The Broadway, c. 1910. The remains of Thatcham's old market cross are still preserved on this spot.

The Broadway, looking west into Church Gate, c. 1910. 'The Old Courthouse' is on the left.

The Broadway, looking towards the High Street, on the occasion of the great snowstorm of 26 April 1908.

Chapel Street, also depicting the day of the great snowstorm in 1908.

The Broadway, showing the snowscape which lasted several weeks during the hard winter of 1962/3.

The Broadway, looking into Church Gate, during the same hard winter.

High Street, looking west from the roof of the White Hart pub, 1963.

The Broadway, looking east around the Broadway Corner from the same high vantage point, 1963.

The Broadway, looking south from the High Street, 1963. Note the public toilets (left), demolished in 1969.

Chapel Street, looking west outside 'Turnfield' Recreation Ground, 1963. This is now the junction with the Moors relief road.

Two

Faces and Places

The Thatched Cottages, c. 1920. Numbers 66-74 Chapel Street still stand as a reminder of the days when many of Thatcham's buildings would have had thatched roofs. Dating from the seventeenth century they were originally charity cottages; after renovation in 1930 they were rented to poor families. Between 1973 and 1974 the five cottages were converted into four and sold into private ownership.

Above: The Thatched Cottages, prior to sale into private ownership. Mrs Steer stands at the door of 66 Chapel Street.

Left: Mr and Mrs Ernest Steer at the door of their home, *c.* 1970.

The old Wheatsheaf inn before it was rebuilt in 1927. William Hobbs (landlord) stands outside with family and friends.

The new Wheatsheaf inn, decorated for the Silver Jubilee of King George V in 1935. Members of the Thatcham Silver Band stand in front.

The Broadway premises of Wyatt's, Family Butcher, Game Dealer and Poulterer, *c.* 1900.

Wyatt's Cash Meat Stores decorated for the coronation of King George VI in 1937.

No. 35 High Street. Thatcham's post office was located here from 1934. Next door (right) was the Drug and Photographic Store and, to the rear, No. 1 Park Lane (see below).

No. 1 Park Lane, the Ladies and Gents Hairdresser, *c.* 1944. Hairdressers Norah Spear, Reg Chivers and Barbara Vass stand outside.

Above: The Crown public house in the High Street was connected with the old Thatcham brewery. The pub closed in 1954.

Below left: Mr George Owen, seen here on his tricycle, was for sixty years a lay preacher in Thatcham.

Below right: The High Street premises of J. C. Norris, Fishmonger and Fruiterer, c. 1930.

Above left: No. 86 Chapel Street. Mrs Hanson's grocery shop—advertising 'Park Drive' and 'Brasso'—is decorated for the 1935 Silver Jubilee of King George V.

Above right: No. 34 Chapel Street, Bill Nightingale's general store, with his wife Edie at the door. Note the advertisements for 'Fry's Chocolate' and 'Lipton's Tea'.

Right: 'Gentleman Jim', James Matthews, outside his grocery shop in Chapel Street in the 1930s.

Thatcham Fruit and Flower Gardens, c. 1915. The 'French' gardens were kept by Miss Hughes-Jones and students from all over the country.

No. 35 Henwick Lane. The smallholding kept by Albert and Alice Webb behind their house, Westview, c. 1920.

Broadway Cycle Shop. These were the premises from which Mr C.G. Brown (originally a watchmaker) was selling cycles by the early 1900s.

The Broadway. The premises of the shop kept by Mr Wilfrid Fuller, Cycle Agent, are shown here with members of the Guild Cycle Club outside in 1919.

No. 10 Chapel Street, the cycle shop kept by Mr Leslie Gilbert from 1931 (above and below left). He also sold wireless and gramophone equipment. Bottom right: Miss Bessie Broughton being presented with a radio by Mr Gilbert.

No. 50 Chapel Street, the hardware store—known as the 'Dinky Stores'—kept by Mr Fred Joyce, decorated for the 1935 Silver Jubilee of King George V. Fred delivered goods locally on his trade bike.

Mr Heath, delivering logs on his donkey cart, poses for the cameraman at the top of Park Lane in 1934.

Mr George Lake, Thatcham chimney sweep and lay preacher, is pictured with Tom, the pony, and cart.

Above left: In old age George 'Sooty' Lake used a tricycle to travel around the locality in the course of his work.

Above right: George's son, Arthur (a gamekeeper) poses at the Swan around 1935 with a large pike he had caught in the Kennet.

Right: Another keen angler, Malcolm Langford, photographed around 1960 with a trout fished from the Kennet.

Station Road Corner. This house (now demolished) stood in front of Brown's turnery, and was occupied by the caretaker.

The Broadway. This building was Thatcham's old workhouse and was demolished in 1959 to make way for the Tanner House shops.

Broadway Corner. These premises fell victim to the new relief road in 1962. The square building was Reg Smart's chip shop.

Bluecoat School. Still standing after nearly seven hundred years, the school building (1707–1914) was originally a chapel, built c. 1304.

No. 102 Chapel Street. Better known as Marsh House, this fine residence was built in the eighteenth century. Although designated a listed building, the old house suffered the same fate as many others in Thatcham, being demolished in 1972. This photograph of the house was taken around 1960.

Three

Schooldays

Francis Baily School, originally Thatcham's 'Council School', built in 1913. The school received the appellation Francis Baily in 1964, after the celebrated astronomer, whose family lived in Thatcham in the eighteenth century and who was buried in the parish church when he died in 1844. In this view from the late 1960s, Miss G. M. Lawrence's class are hard at work.

Above: Bluecoat School boys gather outside their school in the early years of this century. The school was a charity school, opened in 1707 and closed in 1914.

Left: A rare photograph of a bluecoat boy in close-up. The uniform consisted of blue coats and stockings with leather breeches—the latter were apparently very uncomfortable to sit in when hastily dried after a soaking in the rain!

Park Lane School. Looking north up Park Lane the school is on the right. It opened as a National (Anglican) school in 1846.

The school football team of 1930/1. Back row, left to right: Mr Chapman (teacher), J. Wise, W. Goodman, C. Chamberlain. Middle row: A. Fowler, W. Vallance, A. Amor. Front row: M. Richardson, C. Muttram, A. Blissett, B. Claridge, B. Holland.

Pupils of Park Lane School, c. 1932. Back row, left to right: Henry Stacey, John Smith, Cyril Bartholomew, -?-, Ray Rogers, Mick Fowler, Charlie Brown, Freddie Dewdney. Middle row: Rose Goodman, -?-, Sidney McBain, Bobby East, Don Tigwell, Bert Worthy, Win Slade. Front row: Peggy Holland, -?-, Monica Willis, Flossie Goodyear, Nancy French, -?-, ? Muttram.

Pupils of Park Lane School, c. 1948. Back row, left to right: Bill Spriggs, John Grover, Dave Collins, Dennis Muttram, Geoff Smart, Rodney Gray, George Fuller, Jimmy Collins, Robin Morris. Second row: -?-, ? Whale, ? Taylor, ? Elliott, ? Blundy, ? Weisman, Denise Taylor, Shirley Rabbetts, Jean Gall, Betty Tanner. Third row: Ray Chandler, Andy Tuttle, Bryn Lawrence, Graham Bailey, Bobby Lawes. Front row: Roy Tubb, Ernie Steer, Gordon Wilkins, David Downes, Mick Smith, Don Stacey, Bernie Hull, Teddy Mann, Cliff Munday.

Pupils of Church Lane School, photographed around 1900 with Mr H. B. Skillman, headmaster from 1882 until 1913 when the school closed. He transferred to the Council School, and was headmaster there until 1922.

Pupils of Church Lane School which functioned as a 'British' (Nonconformist) school from 1847 until 1913.

A teacher and her pupils—identified as class 'Standard II'—outside Church Lane School, 12 March 1908.

Class of 1909 at Church Lane School, with teachers Miss Kate Hyde (left) and Miss Rhoda Pearce (right).

Broadway Infant's School. Pupils of Thatcham's Church of England Infant's School are photographed here with teacher Mrs Pocock in 1938.

A group of pupils of the Infant's School photographed in the 1950s. The school itself opened in 1828 and closed in 1964.

The Council School, built on a new site in London Road. It opened in 1913 to succeed Church Lane School.

Pupils and teachers Rhoda Pearce (left) and Miss Minnie Pearce of the Council School in March 1920.

The Council School's Class I (oldest children), c. 1927. Mr Cox (headmaster) is standing at the back, third from left, with pupil teachers Misses Stanbrook and Hart and Arthur Collins.

The school's Class IV at about the same date, with teachers Miss E. Hart (left) and Miss D. King (right).

A Council School class photograph from 1929, with teachers Miss G. M. Lawrence (left) and Miss E. Pinnock (right).

Another picture from the summer of 1929: an infant class with teacher Miss Downton (later Mrs Ingram).

A Council School class of 1927. Pupils include: (back row) Frank Keylock, William Carter, Gladys Wickens; (middle row) Bernard Randall; (front row) Arthur Collins, Wilfred Rutter, Pat French.

The school's Class II in 1930, with teacher Mr Reg Taylor. Pupils include: (back row) Doug Durbidge, Roy Joyce; (second row) Ron Durbidge, Dick Corps, Mary Arnold, Ivy Stacey; (front row) George Diplock, Lillian Haines, Joan Collins.

The Council School's Class Ib in 1931. It is thought that the teacher here may be Miss Edwards. Pupils include Bill Marshall (front row, right).

The school's Class I in 1932, with Mr Cox (headmaster). Pupils include: (second row) Rose Cooper, Winnie Durham, Kenneth Adams, Olive Gilmour, Ruth Collins; (front row) Dennis Crees, Edith Headlong (holding board), Doris Franklin.

May Day, 1931. Pupils of the Council School perform a May Day celebration in the playground, directed by teacher Miss Peters.

May Day, 1929. As part of the same event a couple of years earlier a procession of garlanded girls is led by the May Queen.

Coronation Day, 1937. The girls of the Council School surround five-year-old June Patterson, elected the 'Coronation Queen'.

Coronation Day, 1937. The boys of the Council School play their part on the great day by forming a 'Coronation Band'.

Coronation Day, 1937. 'Queen' June Patterson's attendants include (left to right): Dulcie Haines, Muriel Halfacree, Doris Ralph, Valerie Smythe, Audrey Walker, Margaret Hemmings, Dorothy Goodman, Barbara Lugg, Edna Giggs, Monica Worthy, Dorothy Giggs, Barbara Ralph, Elizabeth Brown and Marion Lawrence.

Coronation Day, 1937. Pupils of the Council School rehearse their maypole dance, prior to performing on the Broadway Green.

The Council School's football team in 1948, with teachers Mr Laurie Turner (left) and Mr Douglas Dominey (right). Players include Les Whincup, Dennis Powers and Alan Owen.

The school's football team, in a different strip for the 1951/2 season, again with teacher Mr Laurie Turner. Players include Sid Tyler, Dennis Wheeler and Michael Aldridge.

The Kennet School, opened in 1957 as Thatcham's first purpose-built secondary school. The staff featured in this 1961 group photograph are (left to right): Lillian Curtis (senior mistress), George Hurford (headmaster, 1961–78), Dennis Egginton (deputy head), Lyn Jones (Mathematics), Paul Markham (English), Sid Bulbeck (Technical Studies), Robert Bilsbury (Music).

Boys of the Kennet School in 1961 with male staff including Matt Stratton, Algy Basham, Chris Smith, John Crowther, Roy Monkcom, Bill Prosser, Garth Freeman and Dave Watton.

Girls of the Kennet School in 1961 with female staff including Freda Poole, Pauline Cornell, Ruth Webber, Jessie Hanson, Ann Sharples, Wendy Bassom and Violet Hibberd.

Ex-Council School staff Mr H.B. Skillman (retired in 1922), Miss Eleanor Pinnock and Miss Hettie Peters.

The staff of the Council School in 1954. Back row: Miss Lawrence, Mr Graham, Mr Vicarage, Mr Norwood, Mr Malcolm, Mrs Pocock. Front row: Miss Hargreaves, Mrs Towers, Mr Domoney (headmaster), Mrs Brown, Mrs Hibberd.

Four

Working World

For most of its long history Thatcham has been an agricultural community. Wood-turning and paper-making were established by the eighteenth century, with other industries developing in later years. This picture, dating from the 1930s, is a reminder of Thatcham's farming past, showing haymaking in progress at what is now Brownsfield (site of the council offices).

At the meadow (now Brownsfield) Mr Cooper, employee of Woodbridge's farm, drives a horse-drawn mower around 1937.

At the same time and place the hay is piled into a rick, supervised by farmer Frank Woodbridge (on top of the rick).

Hatchgate Farm on the Cold Ash road, c. 1890. Farmer Ted Matthews can be seen with his sister outside the farmhouse.

Another photograph taken at Hatchgate Farm with employee Mr Headlong leading out one of the farm's horses.

The only known photograph (c. 1924) of the Whitelands Farm brick kiln. This is now the site of Parkside Road.

An early view of the turnery established by Messrs Browns at a small works at the Station Road end of Turnfields.

The turnery works of Messrs Collins and Witts, established behind the parish hall in 1919, following a disastrous fire in 1932—the traction engine seems to have been acquired from Messrs Browns.

The proprietor's son, Aubrey Collins, surveys the ruined turnery. The business later moved to St John's Road.

Looking north from the Moors around 1920, these were the premises of John Brown & Sons, established in 1847.

The turnery from the front around the same date. The employee on the left may be a foreman.

Another view of the turnery and employees, c. 1920. The proprietors were Mr T.H. Brown (left) and Mr A. Brown (right).

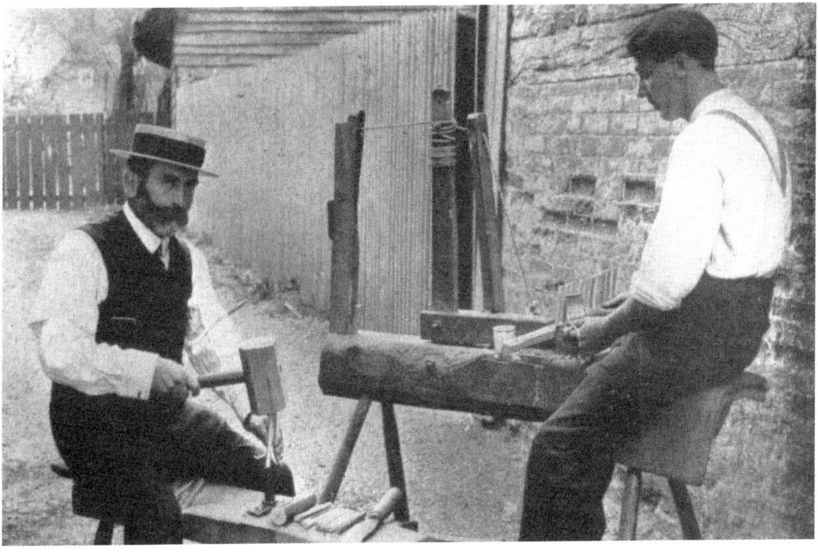

Mr Brown and Mr Wells (employee) making and fitting teeth for hay rakes, c. 1910.

More views from around 1910. Employees de-bark the timber so that it dries and seasons more quickly.

The turnery specialized in rakes and mop handles. Here, stakes for handles are cut to length and stacked.

After the mop handles have been cleaned and partially shaved up, employee Mr Smith straightens them.

As the last stage in mop handle manufacture, Mr Smith rounds them off with a revolving plane.

Above: Employees Mr Charles Clark and Mr Harry Wells assemble hay rakes.

Below left: Mr Wallington knocks in rake teeth.

Below right: Mr George Durbidge works at his lathe at the turnery.

A later photograph (c. 1950) of Brown's turnery. Following a fire in February 1949 the factory was renovated and this rack-saw bench was installed. The rack-saw is operated by Mr Tigwell (left) and Mr Bert Haines (right).

The employees of Brown's coach and van works outside the workshop, c. 1920. Mr C.G. Brown is on the left.

Brown's garage premises had previously been a smithy; the old forge and 'tyring ring' are visible.

ENBORNE
ENGINEERING CO.
(Incorporating T.W.CROWN)
OFFICE.

Enborne Engineering staff. The firm operated at the rear of Brown's garage during the 1960s.

Staff of the (now demolished) Central Depot in Green Lane where school meals were prepared from 1944 until 1965.

Lady driver and cooks pose with depot butcher Trevor Gaunt in front of one of the delivery vans in May 1945.

Driver Mrs Jean Donnelly with one of the depot's vans in 1947. Forty schools were served with two thousand meals prepared in the depot kitchen.

Painting, not cooking, during the summer holiday, 1946. Included here are Gloria Goodman, Molly Rampton, Anne McAvey and Winnie Ainsworth.

Colthrop Mill. The canal-side mill began making paper around 1744. This is the South (old) Mill as it was around 1920.

A unique photograph of the South Mill's steam engine in the charge of Mr Charles Lovegrove around 1920.

In recent times one of Colthrop Mill's cardboard forming moulds (a mesh covered roller) receives maintenance.

The mill once had its own railway sidings and a diesel shunting locomotive named *Churchill*, pictured here in 1962.

A works outing (c. 1950) featuring the manager of Colthrop Mill, Mr Morrison, and Messrs Cyril and Alfie Muttram, Pete Worthy, Harold Lovelock, Stan Baker and Bernard Wallington.

The pulp shed in the early 1950s with employees including Nat Aldridge, Charlie Smith, Mick Hunt, Paddy Oswald, Ken Moore and Terry Hartnett.

Colthrop Mill fire brigade in the late 1950s. On display are trophies won in competitions. The officers include John Henry (managing director) and Stan Langford (chief fire officer).

A fire in the rag store in the 1950s is tackled by the mill fire brigade. The men's wives serve them tea!

The exterior of Thatcham's last woodturnery, established in St John's Road in 1959 by Collins and Witts.

Employee Mr Alf Wallington using a belt-driven lathe to turn handles for paint and glue brushes.

Above left: De-barking logs on a large rotary cutter.

Above right: Turning brush handles on a semi-automatic lathe.

Below: Employee Mr Arthur Crook trimming brush stocks by hand.

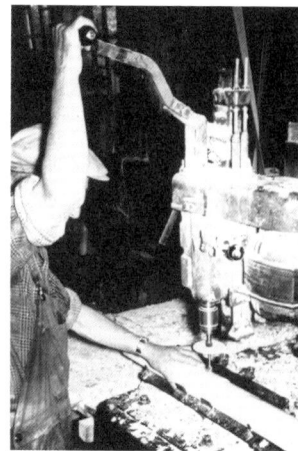

Above left: Cutting logs in half to make broom heads.

Above right: Drilling holes in broom heads for the handles.

Below: Employee Mr Bert Nightingale 'black Japanning' brush stocks, prior to 'stoving' them overnight in an oven.

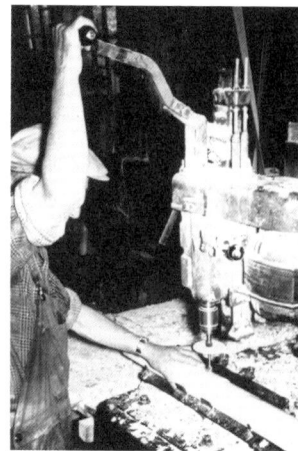

Five

Road, Rail and Canal

The toll-house (right) where the Thatcham turnpike gate once stood, *c.* 1955. The road through Thatcham was turnpiked around 1720 as the Theale–Newbury section of the Bath Road. The railway came to Thatcham in 1847 as a branch line from Reading to Hungerford (and became the main line through to the West Country in 1906).

Charabanc outing, early 1920s. Those on board include Mr and Mrs Charles Lyford (front centre, both in hats), Olive Lyford (back row, second from right), Fred Farley and George Ralph (in sailor uniform).

Charabanc outing, late 1920s. Far left: Mr and Mrs Harry Goodman. Standing, centre: Jack Hill. Standing, right: Alice Mace. Seated, centre: Mr and Mrs Broughton.

Members of St Mary's church choir on an outing, c. 1930. Left to right they include: Mr and Mrs Fyfield, Eva Fyfield, Miss Cousens, Joan Staccini, Ron Hale (hatless), Wilf Phillips, Mr Legge.

Bright Hour outing. Members of this Methodist church group include Mrs Matilda Bosley, Percy Bosley (open jacket), Mrs Edith Collins and daughter Ruth, and twins Joy and Margaret Denness.

Road accident. The Broadway Corner claimed many victims, such as this car which crashed into C. G. Brown's shop around 1920.

A Thatcham Road Transport Services steam lorry on its way to London ended up in a trench beside the A4 in July 1929.

Another victim of the Broadway Corner was this Guinness tanker which crashed in the High Street in March 1954.

The tanker demolished the front of the White Hart and flooded the pub's cellar with 1,000 gallons of stout!

A wintry scene at the top of Park Lane in January 1933 with only a solitary motor vehicle in sight.

Park Lane, looking from the High Street around 1960, before the relief road was built across it.
The barn (right) was demolished to make way for the new road.

Broadway Corner. Another view just pre-dating the relief road. Ignoring the style of the car, the date is around 1960.

High Street, near the premises of F. J. Reynolds Ltd, c. 1961. The relief road was built through here and opened in 1962.

Thatcham station, looking west, in 1920. Mr Leslie White awaits a train to London, *en route* to Australia!

The station from the old footbridge, looking east, with a steam train passing, *c.* 1960.

The old station, looking west, in the early 1960s. The long-gone goods shed is on the left.

The old footbridge (demolished in 1965) and the old-style level-crossing gates (replaced by new style lifting barriers in 1978).

A track-level view, looking east, showing the old station buildings which were demolished in November 1965.

The station from the old footbridge, showing the semaphore signals replaced by multiple aspect signalling (i.e. coloured lights) in 1977–8.

Thatcham signal-box, opened in April 1921 to replace an earlier box which stood on the other side of the tracks, was demolished in May 1978. Signalman P. Kelly inspects the flooding caused by a downpour of summer rain in June 1971.

The Kennet and Avon Canal. The River Kennet was first made navigable between Reading and Newbury. This involved the making of eleven miles of 'cuts' to bypass the meanders of the river, thus creating the Kennet Navigation which opened in 1723. Later, the Kennet Navigation was linked to the Avon Navigation at Bath by the Kennet and Avon Canal; this linked Reading and Bristol, and opened in 1810. However, the canal's life was curtailed by the arrival of the Great Western Railway which bought the waterway in 1852 only to run it down. Several sections of the canal became impassable and it was only fully reopened in 1991. At the time of this view, around 1910, there was still an interchange of goods (rolls of paper from Colthrop Mill) between canal and rail, via the wharf adjacent to the goods yard at Thatcham station.

The bottom gates of Monkey Marsh Lock, 1906. This was one of the Navigation's original turf-sided locks.

The top gates of Monkey Marsh Lock in the 1960s. By this date the lock was derelict.

Bulls Lock, Newbury, *c.* 1904. The lengthman's house to the right of the lock was demolished around 1946.

Ham Mills, *c.* 1906. This was part of Thatcham parish until 1891 and perhaps the site of one of Thatcham's Domesday mills.

Six

Sport and Leisure

Sporting activities must have been a part of village life in Thatcham for centuries but organized sport has proliferated only in the last hundred years. The Thatcham Cycling Club was formed in May 1892 with the enrolment of eighteen members. There were weekly rides to places such as Brimpton and Crookham. Other organized activities included football, cricket and opera. Thatcham Football Club was founded in 1906. The team won the Senior Cup in the Reading Challenge Cup Competition in the 1935/6, 1947/8, 1949/50, and 1950/1 seasons. Thatcham Cricket Club was founded in 1919 and originally played on The Marsh. Thatcham's Amateur Operatic Society, Ye Ancient Britons, was established around 1923.

Thatcham Lads Football Club team, 1913/14. The goalkeeper was Leonard Durbidge.

Thatcham FC team, 1919/20. Back row, second from right: Richard White. Front row, second from right: Albert Nightingale.

Thatcham FC team, 1935/6. Centre: Cyril Barr (capt.). Front row, right: Less Attfield (goalkeeper).

The first Thatcham Minors team, 1937/8. Back row: Freddy Davies, Charlie Seymour, Ken Bartholomew, Jack Davies, Les Arnold, Gordon Barr, Bert Parker. Middle row: Peter House, Jack Brooks, George Slade (capt.), Percy Davies, Stan Dennis. Front row: Max Goddard, Russell Hunt.

Thatcham FC first team, c. 1960. Cyril Bartholomew and Reg Taylor (left) and Bill Fry, Harry Brown and Birt Claridge (right). Players include: (back row) Dennis Wheeler, John Mann (goalkeeper), Ray Chandler; (front row) Keith Armstrong, Jim Vallis and Clifford Fry.

Thatcham Minors team, 1963/4. Players include: (back row) Eddie Denness (trainer), Malcolm Broughton, Leon Sheldon, Colin Fox, Dennis Keylock, Joe Freeman, Dennis Keogh; (front row) Colin Young, Bernard Keylock, Vic Pye, Tony Ayres, Mick Dunbar, Chris Doyle.

The start of the first Vic French Memorial Trophy match held around 1960: 'old players' versus the current team.

Participants in the Memorial match included John Holbon (referee), 'Digger' Blisset, Billy Wilkins, Jock Hutchinson, Norman Hall, Jack Brooks, Percy Davies, Jim Thirkill, Jack Davies, John Lloyd, Bob Smith, Eric Fisher, David Molloy, Cyril Bartholomew, Sam Aldridge, George Slade, Gordon Bowden, Birt Claridge.

Cricket Club, c. 1920. The umpire (back row, right) is Reg Durbidge. Players include George Davies, Les Mason, George Harris, Harry Pearson, Oliver Rich and Bill Oram (boy on right).

Cricket Club, c. 1930. Back row, left to right: ? Haines (umpire), Sidney Ashman, Stanley Brown, Capt. Webb, Bill Clippendale, Ray Onion, Howard Peters, Tommy Fisher (scorer).
Front row: Max Langdon, Cyril Barr, Jim Vallis, Bobby Brown, Fred Davis.

Thatcham Cricket Club's 2nd XI for the 1948 season. Back row, left to right: John Holbon, Cyril Bartholomew, Eric Eastman, Peter House, Jack Brooks, Richard Watts, John Wimbush, 'Tankie' Smith. Front row: Owen Digweed, Ross Arnold, Max Langdon, Charlie Smith, Jack Wheeler, Bernard Spanswick.

Cricket Club, c. 1960. Back row, left to right: John Holbon (umpire), Harry Barrett, Johnny Mann, Barry Dolton, Harry Tweedy, John Wimbush, Gordon Barr, Norman Peel. Front row: Sidney Norwood, Peter Holloway, Jack Brooks, Percy Davies, Clifford Fry. Boy at front: Keith Davies.

Thatcham Ladies' Football Team, 1954. Trainer: Mr Fred Cripps. Players include Brenda Witts, Phyllis Worthy, Dora Dennis, Doris Goodman, Vera Worthy, Beryl Spriggs, Pat Lovelock.

Thatcham Boys' Club Football Team, c. 1950s. Trainer: Charlie Denness. Players include Harry Barrett, Keith Rumble, Bill Morris, Peter Stanbrook, Mickey Collins, Malcolm Passey.

St Mary's School Cricket Club, c. 1948. Back row, left to right: Bill Spriggs, Mr Marriott (teacher), Andy Tuttle, Rodney Gray, Robin Andrews, Ernie Steer. Front row: Douglas Collins, Gordon Wilkins, Robin Morris, John Mann, Richard Down, Ray Chandler, David Down.

Amateur Operatics. The cast of *Highwayman Love*, performed by Ye Ancient Britons in April 1928. Front row, centre: Mr Sidney Ashman (hon. sec.) and his wife, Mrs Munro Ashman.

The 'Ancient Britons', c. 1930. This group includes Frank Ashman, Wilf Phillips, Madge Gooding, Bill Hall, Gertie Collins, Evelyn Durbidge and musical director Miss K. Carter.

The Thatcham Amateur Variety Artistes performing *Babes in the Wood* in January 1952, with Valerie Hawkins and Peggy Slade as the 'babes'.

Performed at the British School, the TAVA Christmas pantomime in January 1954 was *Aladdin*. The lead role was played by Barbara Gough, with Sheila Powell as the princess. The musicians are, from left to right: Jack Whiting (drums), Michael Huntley (piano accordion), Derek Goddard (saxophone), Ted Turner (piano), Ann Monaghan (dance teacher), Fred Goddard (violin) and Sybil Goddard (cello).

Members of the Silver Band, including bandmaster Mr W. Woodward (with baton) and Mr and Mrs John Henry, c. 1927.

The band came second in its section at Alexandra Palace in September 1937. Members include Ted Buckle, Seth Townsend, Cyril Rutter, Charlie Packer, Bill Hall, Reg Durbidge, Ashley Gunter, Jim Smith, Stan Eggleton, Jessie Chilton, Jim Cope.

Members of the Old Folks' Choir at the Parish Hall in August 1955. The conductor was Mrs Smith.

The Christmas show at the Parish Hall in December 1958, where the choir performed the *Gypsy Encampment*.

The centenary of the founding of John Brown & Sons' woodturnery, in October 1947. The anniversary was celebrated at a dinner and entertainment which the directors gave their seventy employees, their wives and guests at the British School. Three generations of the Brown family were present, with Mr A.B.V. Brown presiding centre, nearest the camera. In recognition of their long service, cheques were presented to Harry House, Tom Collins, Harry Chandler, Tom Denness, Joe Franklin, Charlie Denness and Jack Randall, who had all completed fifty or more years with the firm.

Seven

Special Occasions

In old Thatcham, most special events were based either on the Broadway Green or the parish church, as the following sequence of photographs shows. To mark special occasions the tradition in Thatcham was to fire an 'anvil salute'. The first recorded salute was for Queen Victoria's coronation in 1837, but the custom probably originated much earlier. The last time anvils were fired in Thatcham was on the occasion of the Thatcham Festival in June 1970. This photograph depicts a quieter event, a 'Camp Meeting' on the Broadway Green around 1900. It seems to have been connected with the summer camps arranged by the local churches.

The parish church showing the location of the family tomb of the Tull family at the base of the tower.

The funeral procession of 'Squire' A.R. Tull of Crookham House, arriving at the church in November 1914.

Squire Tull's coffin is preceded by Revd Edward Chamberlain. Mr A.S.B. Tull (son and heir) is following.

Seen from the tower, a large assemblage of mourners observe the burial of Squire Tull in the family vault.

Thatcham's war memorial, originally located in the Broadway, was unveiled on Armistice Day, November 1920.

General Dickson (Royal Berks Regt) steps forward to unveil the memorial as Major Turner unveils the gun.

The field gun was a German howitzer captured in the First World War and presented to Thatcham by the War Office.

Flowers and wreaths are placed on the memorial by women and girls including Mrs Turner and Miss Gertie Bosley.

The parish church. The present parish church of St Mary was built around 1141, although the edifice was extensively restored between 1857 and 1858. The Norman doorway is virtually all that remains of the original twelfth-century building following the Victorian restoration. In this view, from around 1930, the Tull tomb is clearly visible. The gate in the foreground leads into the field where Meadow Close was built in the 1960s.

St Mary's church choir in 1932, with Revd MacWilliam (curate), Mr Brown (verger), and Mr Fyfield (organist).

The boys of the choir in 1933, with Revd MacWilliam and Mr Rowles (vicar's warden). It looks like Palm Sunday.

The view in Church Gate (looking east) when the churchyard was enclosed by a six-foot-high wall. The wall was reduced to three feet to improve road visibility in 1936.

A new timber framework constructed in 1934 to replace worm-eaten roof timbers in the church's Danvers' Chapel.

Above: The view in Church Gate (looking west) in 1934, again showing the high churchyard wall, and a long-gone gas lamp!

Right: Repair work, undertaken by local builder Mr W. Legge, in progress on the roof of the Danvers' Chapel in 1934.

Above: Patriotic decorations are displayed in St John's Road to celebrate the Silver Jubilee of King George V in 1935.

Below left: The traditional penny-farthing was made by Mr Tom Ryan in 1935.

Below right: Crowds line the High Street waiting for the carnival procession.

![above image]

Above: Decorated trade vehicles form up for the carnival procession.

Below left: A private car, registration JB 1688, joins the procession.

Below right: The procession moves off from the Broadway around the village.

Above: Coronation Day, 1937 started in Thatcham with an open air service in the Broadway, conducted by Revd A. O. Daniel.

Below left: Speeches from the platform were aided by a public address system.

Below right: King George VI's speech from London was relayed to the crowd by loudspeakers.

Watched by the Broadway crowd, village doctor James Beagley crowns Miss Winifred Hall 'Queen of the May'.

The May Queen, attended by her maids of honour, then toured the village on the back of a lorry loaned by TRTS.

Home Guard. In May 1940 Anthony Eden called on men aged between 17 and 65 who were
not engaged in military service (because of their age, infirmity or 'reserved occupation') to
join a Local Defence Volunteer Force. By July, when the name of the force was changed to the
Home Guard, recruitment had to be suspended because over 1,300,000 men had enrolled.
The Home Guard was Britain's part-time army. The South Midland Home Guard Transport
Column, based in Oxford but with a depot in Thatcham, was made up of local men plus drivers
from Abingdon, Reading and Oxford. A local man, Wilfrid Street (co-founder of Thatcham
Road Transport Services), became Lieutenant-Colonel of the column, commanding a wide area.
There were about 200 men in the Home Guard's TRTS division alone. The Thatcham depot
was based at the premises of TRTS at Colthrop. Among the men in this photograph of the
Thatcham Home Guard are: (back row) Ernie Brown, Stan Diver; (second row) Sam Aldridge,
George Worthy, Jim Cramb, Harry Pemberton, Ted Gaul, Ted Wheeler, John Denness, Charlie
Hyde, Norman Wheeler, John Hunt, William Diggins; (third row) Fred Rosier, Frederick Mecey
(officer i/c), Bill Fitch; (front row) Fred Farley, Stan Blandford, Jimmy Hanson, Joe Mace,
Ernie Slade, Johnny Wimbush.

A group of Thatcham ARP wardens and messengers at John Brown & Sons woodturnery in 1943. Back row, left to right: Fred Chandler, Tom Jacobs, -?-, Mr Cutting, Gilbert Mayhew, Richard Wallington (in 'civvies' because his uniform had not arrived). Middle row: Vincent Brown, Sidney Clark, Norman Pinnock, Mr Crouch, Robert Brown jun., Mr Mortimer, -?-, Frank Mayow, Arthur Brown. Front row: Miss Cecilia Nightingale, Ron Denness, -?-, Robert Brown sen. (head warden), George Barrett, Mr Keene, Mrs Holland.

Another group photograph of Thatcham's ARP personnel, this time members of the Rescue Services, at the Grange in August 1943. In the centre of the second row is 'Squire' A.S.B. Tull, who helped to set up the local group. On either side of Mr Tull are Mr and Mrs Tapley, who lived at the Grange and who also organized the unit. Other individuals in the group include: (back row) Basil Pinnock, Ted Thatcher, 'Bill' Fuller; (middle row, standing) Tom King, Margaret Lawrence, Norman Pinnock, Mrs Barker, Cyril Barr, Pearl Lewis, Max Breach; (middle row, seated) Mary Hall, Norman Randall; (front row) 'Tankie' Smith, Ray Rogers, 'Yorkie' Smith, Miss Tapley, Bernard Wallington, Bernard Bowden.

Victory celebration. The inhabitants of the hamlet of Colthrop celebrated VE day in their own special way in May 1945. Among the individuals who can be identified in this picture are, left to right: (back row) Billy Muttram, David Turner, Lilly Gregory, Dolly Denness, Pearl Turner, Mrs Muttram, Mrs Smart, Mrs Piggott, Fred Smart, Tom Blissett; (middle row) Mrs Muttram, Mrs Hayward, Mrs Turner, Mrs Tanner, Mrs Cannings, Kate Taylor, Joyce Turner, Minnie Breach, Geoff Tanner, Len Breach, 'Grandad' Muttram, 'Grannie' Breach; (front row) Ron Tanner (dressed as a girl), Jean Breach, Pam Smart, Sybil Picket (Robin Hood), Maureen Smart (Dolly in the Box), Joyce Vogel, Grace Breach, Raymond Breach.

The residents of St John's Road at their VE day celebration in May 1945, including: (back row) Joyce Hazell, Mrs Baker, Mrs Wheeler, Mrs Slade; (front row) Mrs Hill, Mrs Powell, Mrs French, Mr Hazell, Mrs Berry, Mrs Copping and child, Mrs Salt and child, Mrs Buckland, Mrs Townsend.

The younger residents of St John's Road include: (back row) Ray Berry, Ray Townsend, Ron Townsend, Gil Slade; (middle row) Cynthia Barrett, Joyce Barrett, Eileen Smith, Julie Baker, Audrey Salt, Carol Collins, Ray Wheeler; (front row) Mary Cram, Margaret Smith, Harry Barrett, Tony Powell, Jane Wheeler, Richard Copping, Josephine Copping, Arthur Salt, Ivor Townsend, Dennis Wheeler.

Anvil firing. The ancient custom of firing an anvil salute in the Broadway, here on the coronation of King George VI, 12 May 1937.

The last anvils fired in Thatcham, by Jeff Neal and Laurie Turner, at the Thatcham Festival on 27 June 1970.

The Thatcham Folk Festival, a week-long event, began in the Broadway on the afternoon of Saturday 27 June 1970.

Following the display of anvil firing, pupils from St Mary's and Francis Baily Primary Schools performed folk dances.

The pupils of St Mary's School performed four English country dances.

The pupils of Francis Baily School performed three folk dances, accompanied by recorders and percussion instruments.

Above: Tower restoration. Between 1969 and 1970 the tower of the parish church was renovated. Note that this meant the removal of the pinnacles!

Right: Two new bells were hung in the tower and dedicated to former bell-ringers Arthur Henry Brown and Audrey Butler at a dedication ceremony held on 6 March 1970.

Campanologists. The Band of Bell Ringers at St Mary's church in 1971. Back row, left to right: Jenny Barker; Alan Edens; Richard Butler; Ron Christopher; Reg W. Rex; Graeme Turner; Cyril Tilling; Dennis Muttram; Valerie Edens; Robert Ashman; Mary Stone; Arthur Stacey; George Donkin; Revd Michael Williams. Front row: William Butler (tower captain); Stanley Brown; Fred Marshall; Right Revd Eric Knell, Bishop of Reading; Revd Stanley Cornish; Dr Warwick Brown; Anthony Christopher.

Eight

Around and About

The parish of Thatcham was once much more extensive than it is today. It included places which have now become parishes in their own right, such as Midgham (separated in 1891), Greenham (1891), Cold Ash (1894), and outlying places with identities of their own, such as Colthrop and Crookham. Featured above is Midgham Bridge on the Kennet and Avon Canal, around 1906.

Cold Ash Hill, c. 1915. Collaroy Road can just be seen leading off right. The house in the foreground was demolished around 1970.

St Finian's Farm, c. 1895. Farmer Robert Law milks the cows in the field beside the farmhouse.

Cold Ash Hill, c. 1920. The post office was kept by the Pocock family before the garage opened on the site.

Looking up the hill around 1950 when Mr Walden kept the post office and Norman Pocock ran the garage beyond it.

Cold Ash Hill. The cottages have deeper front gardens today. 'Sudgie' Piper, shoe-repairer, lived in the house (left).

The Castle green, Coldash.

The one-time 'green' outside the Castle pub, c. 1930. The thatched house beyond the green is Ivy Cottage.

Above: The church of St Mark at Cold Ash was built in 1864. It was constructed in fourteenth-century style from red brick with stone dressings and a tiled roof. Seen here around 1930, from the west, the south porch and bellcote (with two bells) are clearly visible.

Right: An interior view of the church, looking east and showing the apsidal chancel from the nave, at around the same date.

The lych-gate at St Mark's church with Cold Ash School (opened 1874) beyond it, c. 1920.

Cold Ash crossroads, looking north, with the same two gentlemen in view, c. 1920. Also note the postman emptying the postbox.

Cold Ash crossroads, c. 1930. The new recreation ground is on the left and the Children's Hospital is in the distance on the right.

COLDASH HOSPITAL.

The Children's Hospital, seen here around 1930, opened in 1892 as a 'cottage hospital' and closed in 1964.

Acland Memorial Hall soon after it opened in 1925 as a memorial to Sir Reginald Acland, who had died the previous year.

The Ridge, c. 1920. Children of the Loveridge family who kept the Pheasant (right), which closed as a public house around 1950.

Above: Cold Ash from the west around 1930, with Spring Cottages in the foreground and The Ridge in the background.

Below left: Cold Ash Road, *c*. 1930.

Below right: Little Lane, Cold Ash.

Greenham Common, c. 1895. The old Basingstoke road used to go straight across the common and there were also many other tracks.

Greenham Common, c. 1895. From 1873 to 1938 the common was owned by the Baxendale family (who sold it to Newbury Council).

Greenham Common, c. 1908. The common was requisitioned as an RAF airfield in 1941 and became a USAF bomber base from 1951.

Greenham Common, c. 1910. This track across the common is now the route of Bury's Bank Road. There is a golf course on the left today.

St Mary's church at Greenham, consecrated by the Bishop of Oxford in October 1876, replaced the old chapel.

The interior of the church: designed by Henry Woodyer, it was built at a cost of £3,455 by Messrs Elliot.

Greenham Lodge, the manor house of the Baxendales. It was built soon after the family acquired the property in 1873.

When sold off in 1937 the manor house first became a boys' school and then an officers' mess for the airbase.

Crookham Hill, looking up the hill in 1906. Lower Lodge is at the entrance to Crookham House. Bury's Bank is to the right.

Crookham House, c. 1908. The house was home to the Tull family, built around 1850 on the site of an earlier residence.

Crookham House. The Tull family were in effect the 'squires' of Thatcham until 1939 when Mr A. S. B. Tull sold off the estate.

Thornford. A view of the old footbridge and ford across the River Enborne at far Crookham, where Berkshire becomes Hampshire.

The peaceful scene on the Kennet and Avon Canal at Colthrop, *c.* 1906. The lady on the towpath is Grace White.

Another peaceful scene on the canal, close to the paper mill, *c.* 1960. The gentleman fishing is Stan Langford.

Although probably better known for its (paper) mill, Colthrop has always been an outlying hamlet within Thatcham parish. The population was never large and mainly comprised those families who lived in Colthrop Cottages beside the canal and, of course, the family which owned the mill, who lived in Colthrop House nearby. There has been a mill at Colthrop since Domesday times. It was originally a grist (corn) mill, but became a fulling (cloth) mill around 1540 and a paper mill around 1740. The paper mill entered a period of growth from 1861 when it was taken over by the Henry family who developed it to the point where it was employing two hundred people by 1905. The Henry family lived in Colthrop House for over eighty years. This photograph from around 1940 shows some of the inhabitants of Colthrop Cottages, including 'Pop' Chivers, Mrs Turner, children Joyce and David Turner, and Mrs Gregory (at back).

Colthrop Cottages in 1906. A small shop was kept in one of them to serve the needs of Colthrop folk.

Colthrop mill in 1907. A swing bridge across the canal linked the cottages with the mill.

Chamberhouse Mill in 1908. Corn was milled at Chamberhouse for almost six hundred years, until 1965.

Chamberhouse Mill in 1916, when it was a working mill. It was converted to private residences around 1970.

Chamberhouse Farm, *c.* 1904. The farm is (like the mill) on a branch of the River Kennet, not the canal.

Widmead Lock on the Kennet and Avon Canal in 1906. Note the bridge, then situated above the lock.

The Bourne, c. 1906. This little bridge carried Lower Way over the Bourne stream, which flows across the Moors to the canal. The two ladies are Esther Brown (sitting) and katie Branson (standing).

Picnicking on the Moors in August 1914. On the right of the group is Mr John Pike, who ran the Broadway drapery.

Village children bathing in the Moor stream, c. 1920. Note the railway and gate at the foot crossing in the background.

Fishing in the Moor stream, c. 1920. The boy (right) is Clifford Fuller whose family kept the Broadway newsagency.

The lane from Thatcham to Chamberhouse fords a stream close to the swing bridge across the canal. Pamela Fuller (sister of Clifford) is in the foreground, c. 1906.

Acknowledgements

Sincere thanks to all those people who contributed towards this compilation of photographs. Without their assistance the selection available to me would have been less comprehensive and less interesting. For allowing me free access to their cherished private collections, and for providing much information to help me to write captions, I am deeply indebted to the following individuals:

Mrs Rose Bellis • Mr Robert Brown • Mr David Canning • Mrs B. Child
the late Mr Birt Claridge • Mr and Mrs David Cooper • Mr Clifford Fuller
the late Mrs Constance Gilbert • Mrs Jan Gray • Mr Gordon Hands
Mr Graham Holbon • Mr John Holbon • Mrs Sue Hopson • Mr John Hutchings
Mr Ron Joyce • Mr Malcolm Langford • Miss Gwen Lawrence • Mr Ron Lovegrove
Miss Anne McAvey • Mr Basil Parsons • Mr Cyril Rutter • Mr Wilfred Rutter
Mr George Slade • Mr Tony Stacey • Mrs Jenny Thornton • Mrs Hilda Warner
Mr and Mrs Ray Wheeler • Mr Stuart Wise
West Berkshire Heritage Service.